AF228949

Gods of Love

IN WORLD MYTHOLOGY

Don Nardo

San Diego, CA

About the Author

Classical historian and award-winning author Don Nardo has written numerous acclaimed volumes about ancient civilizations and peoples. They include more than three dozen overviews of the mythologies of the Sumerians, Babylonians, Egyptians, Greeks, Romans, Persians, Celts, Norse, Native Americans, and others. Nardo, who also composes and arranges orchestral music, lives with his wife, Christine, in Massachusetts.

LIBRARY OF CONGRESS CATALOGING-IN-PUBLICATION DATA

Names: Nardo, Don, 1947- author.
Title: Gods of love in world mythology / Don Nardo.
Description: San Diego, CA : ReferencePoint Press, 2023. | Series: Mythology around the world | Includes bibliographical references and index.
Identifiers: LCCN 2021051894 (print) | LCCN 2021051895 (ebook) | ISBN 9781678202682 (library binding) | ISBN 9781678202699 (ebook)
Subjects: LCSH: Love--Mythology. | Love--Religious aspects. | Gods.
Classification: LCC BL325.L67 N37 2023 (print) | LCC BL325.L67 (ebook) | DDC 398.27/43--dc23/eng/20211223
LC record available at https://lccn.loc.gov/2021051894
LC ebook record available at https://lccn.loc.gov/2021051895

CONTENTS

Timeless, Universal Tales of Love

In the mid-500s BCE, long before the rise of the Roman Empire, an ambitious Persian prince named Cyrus founded an empire in what is now Iran. The Persian Empire quickly expanded across the Middle East and beyond. Until it was conquered by the Greek king Alexander III (later called "the Great") in the late 300s BCE, the Persian realm was by far the biggest empire in the world. Even after that imperial state's demise, Persian beliefs, culture, and traditions survived.

The Perfect Couple

Like other peoples throughout history, the Persians had, and still have, a number of ancient myths connected to their religion and cultural lore. One of the best-known and most beloved of those old stories is that of the lovers Zal and Rudabeh. A handsome and physically strong young man, Zal had long heard rumors of the incomparable beauty of Rudabeh, daughter of a local Persian ruler named Karbol. Zal had no idea at that point that the princess had heard similar praises of him, especially regarding his prowess as an athlete and soldier.

The two wanted to meet and for Zal to formally court her so that they could eventually marry. However, the heads of the two families were against such a union. In particular, Rudabeh's royal father did not view *any* man as worthy of his precious daughter. So for a while there appeared to be no chance of a romance.

The forthright and bold Zal refused to accept the situation, however. He traveled to King Karbol's palace and asked to speak to the monarch in person. While the young man was waiting for an audience, Rudabeh heard about his arrival and sent three of her female servants to Zal to arrange a secret meeting. The servants told Zal that the princess was heavily guarded day and night. Thus, he should wait till after sundown and sneak to the base of her castle tower. There, she would let her long hair down, and he could use it to climb up to her.

The hair-climbing proved unnecessary, however, for the enterprising Zal brought a sturdy rope with him. As told by the medieval Persian writer Ferdowsi, he "made a running knot, and threw it upwards and fastened it to the battlements." With a romantic and athletic flourish, "he swung himself upon the roof. Then Rudabeh took his hand,"[1] and together they entered the bedchamber in the tower's pinnacle.

Having finally met face-to-face, the two young people instantly fell deeply in love and promised that they would remain in each other's hearts ever after. Moreover, when their parents saw the two together and realized what a perfect couple they made, they relented and gave their blessings for a marriage. The wedding ceremony lasted a full thirty days and was said to be the finest in Persian history. In the fullness of time, Zal succeeded to the kingdom's throne, and he "administered [the government] with wisdom and judgment," Ferdowsi wrote. Furthermore, "Rudabeh sat beside him on the throne, and he placed a crown of gold upon her head."[2]

The Beauty and Purity of Love

Love and lovers are not the only themes in the large collection of surviving Persian myths. Just as the famous ancient Greek myths feature tales of heroes slaying monsters and of humans interacting with divine powers, so too Persian mythology is replete with such stories. In fact, nearly all the national mythologies of people around the globe explore certain universal themes. Among the most common examples are stories about the creation of the world and human race, the way humans are subject to nature's destructive powers, and the inevitability of death for all living things (except for the gods).

Similarly, love has always been viewed as an inevitable and worldwide phenomenon, one that many people over the centuries have thought makes life worth living. The story of Zal and Rudabeh is therefore far from unusual in the world's collected myths. The ancient Egyptians, Greeks, Romans, Chinese, Hindus, and numerous others all celebrated the beauty and purity

The ancient Persians did not have a specific deity associated mainly with love, as the Greeks and many other past peoples did. This is because the Persians were monotheistic. Hence, they tended to look to their sole god, Ahura-Mazda (pictured) for guidance in matters of love.

of true love between spouses, parents and children, siblings, and friends alike. More often than not, such feelings were thought to be the gift of gods and goddesses who oversaw the process of love.

For the Greeks, those deities were Aphrodite and Eros; whereas the monotheistic Persians looked to their supreme god, Ahura-Mazda, for romantic guidance and inspiration.

Such tales, whether divinely inspired or not, are both timeless and universal, says Alia El Saady, a commentator for the Egyptian online magazine *Identity*. "Reflecting on these different stories," she writes, "allows us to truly appreciate the power of love and its ability to transform itself, not only into different kinds but different tales as well, cross culturally and across different timelines. It's interesting to see the ways that love has found the power to endure and to meld into cultures, religions, and histories."[3]

CHAPTER ONE

Ancient Egypt

In one of ancient Egypt's oldest myths, the love that the goddess Isis felt for her divine husband Osiris, overseer of the underworld, was pure, incomparable, and eternal. The two were also sister and brother, and in that tale she fell in love with him when they were fetuses sharing the same womb (that of the sky goddess, Nut). They could not yet see each other. But in ways no one has been able to explain, they could sense each other's presence. And it warmed their hearts to be so near each other.

The same myth pictures Isis as eventually growing up to be a versatile deity seen not only as a protector of women and expert in magic but also as the embodiment of motherhood. For that reason, the Egyptians nicknamed her the "Great Mother." Furthermore, just as mothers are known for the love they feel for their children, Isis harbored a strong love for all Egyptians. That made them, in a sense, her children.

This myth and others about Isis are very old, in large part because Egyptian civilization itself is extremely old. Humans have lived in the Nile River valley for tens of thousands of years. Initially they were nomadic hunter-gatherers, but in about 6000 BCE (roughly eight thousand years ago), they began growing grains and other crops and erecting small permanent villages. Almost all those settlements were situated along the river because once a year it produced mild floods that delivered the water required for large-scale farming.

Over time, the early Egyptians developed a large collection of myths about the many gods they worshipped, including several tales that featured Isis and Osiris. The themes of these stories were diverse. Some gods represented natural phenomena like the sun, moon, seas, and winds, and myths emerged that explained how these things came to be. Similarly, there were gods of death, war, justice, love, and other aspects of the human condition, and there were myths associated with them as well.

In the case of myths about love, certain deities personified that emotion or set examples of loving relationships for humans to follow. Foremost among those divine trendsetters was Isis. A physical description of her—that is, the way the Egyptians and other ancients envisioned her—appears in *The Golden Ass*, a surviving novel by the second-century-CE Roman writer Apuleius. In his words:

> Her lofty head was encircled by a garland interwoven with diverse blossoms. [At their center rested] a flat disk resembling a mirror, or rather the orb of the moon, which emitted a glittering light. The crown was held in place by coils of rearing snakes [and] adorned above with waving ears of corn. She wore a multicolored dress woven from fine linen, one part of which shone radiantly white, a second glowed yellow with saffron blossom, and a third blazed rosy red.[4]

A Deadly Scheme

In addition to the tale of how Isis came to love Osiris in the womb, there was the much more complex story of how her love for him brought about his resurrection from the dead. Often called the

Myth of Kingship, it is both the greatest love story in Egyptian mythology (and possibly all of world mythology) and the most pivotal of all the Egyptian myths. Replete with spiritual, political, and social significance, it strongly influenced Egyptian ideas and customs.

Well before he was resurrected by Isis, the story goes, Osiris was widely seen by all Egyptians as a key fertility god. One of his duties, for instance, was to make the Nile gently flood each year, thereby bringing prosperity to the human community. It was also said that he taught the earliest residents of the Nile valley how to grow crops. These attributes made Osiris widely popular among the early Egyptians, and they were happy to welcome him as their first king.

However, one individual in the kingdom—Osiris's and Isis's bother, Seth—was *not* happy about Osiris's rise to power in Egypt. Seth was both intensely jealous of his royal sibling and power hungry. As a result, Seth secretly concocted a deadly scheme

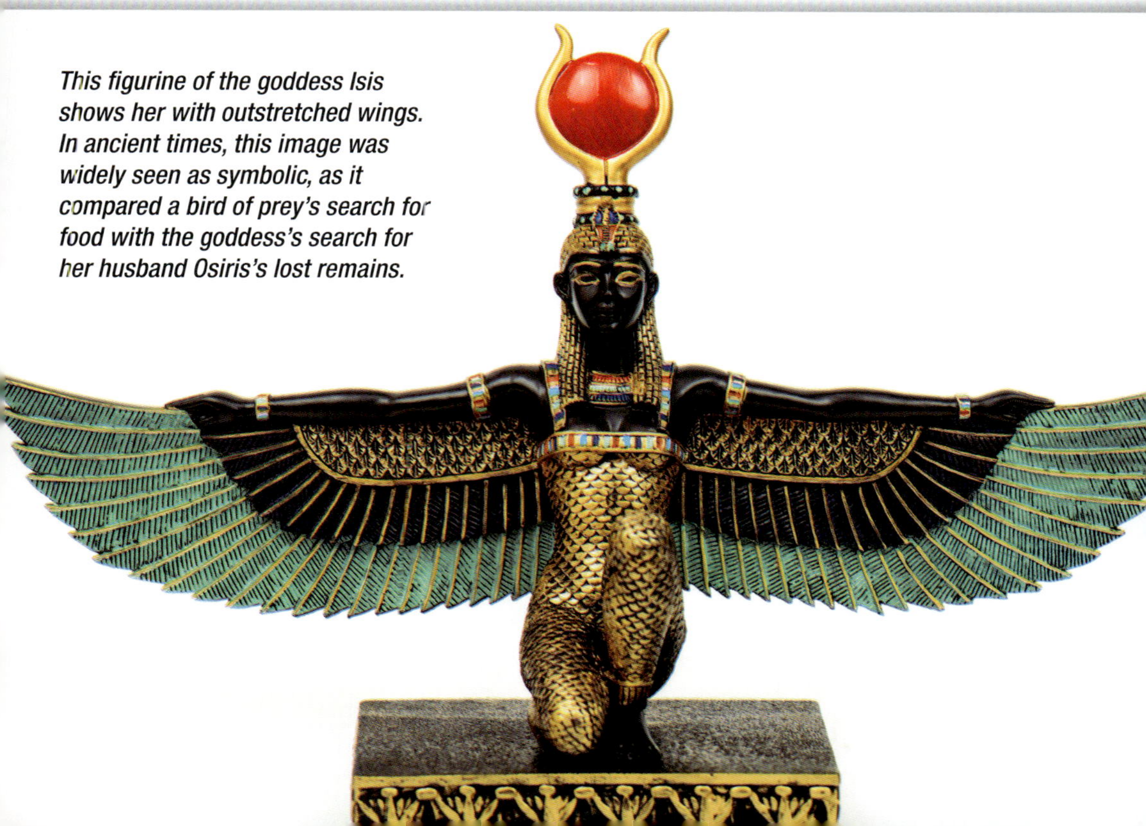

This figurine of the goddess Isis shows her with outstretched wings. In ancient times, this image was widely seen as symbolic, as it compared a bird of prey's search for food with the goddess's search for her husband Osiris's lost remains.

to kill Osiris and seize the throne for himself. The plan began to unfold on a night when Isis was away and the king was having a large-scale feast at the palace for the Egyptian nobles. When Seth himself entered the banquet hall, his servants followed, bearing a big, highly decorated treasure chest.

Seeing the chest, Osiris asked his brother what was inside. Seth replied that at the moment there was nothing inside. Rather, he explained, it was a prop in a special game in which people took turns lying inside the chest. Whoever fit in it most perfectly would be allowed to keep the lovely artifact. One after another the nobles took turns briefly lying inside the chest. Finally, it was the king's turn. What he and the others did not realize was that Seth had made sure beforehand that the chest would conform perfectly to the king's height and contours. Naturally, when Osiris climbed inside, it was a perfect fit.

What happened next was completely unexpected to most of those present. While Osiris reclined in the chest, Seth suddenly slammed the lid down and locked it, trapping the pharaoh inside. As the nobles and servants ran back and forth in fear and confusion, Osiris began gasping from the lack of air in what had become his coffin, and a few minutes later he was dead. Seth then proclaimed himself king, and his first official order was for his guards to carry the chest to the Nile and throw it in.

A Wife's Love and Determination

Very soon after these events occurred, Isis returned and discovered that her beloved husband had been murdered and his throne usurped. Though shocked and filled with grief, she had the presence of mind to initiate a search for her husband's remains. To that end, according to the first-century-CE Greek writer Plutarch, she "wandered everywhere at her wits' end. No one whom she approached did she fail to address, and even when she met

Seth

Brother of Isis and Osiris, he was a divine troublemaker who killed Osiris and usurped Egypt's throne

King Osiris (pictured) is confronted with the box his brother Seth has brought to the banquet in the royal palace. Unbeknownst to the king, Seth plans to trap his brother in the box, which the would-be usurper hopes will become Osiris's coffin.

some little children she asked them about the chest. As it happened, they had seen it, and they told her [to go to] the mouth of the river through which the [followers] of Seth had launched the coffin into the [water]."[5]

Acting on that information, Isis found the chest at the bottom of the river. Hoping to prevent Seth from finding out she had retrieved it, she hid the container in some remote marshes. By chance, however, a few days later one of the new king's followers was out hunting in those same marshes. That individual found the chest and alerted Seth, who proceeded to take an extreme measure. According to Plutarch, he drew his sword and cut up the body into numerous fragments and

> scattered them, each in a different place. Isis learned of this and sought [to find] them . . . sailing through the swamps in a boat of papyrus. This is the reason why people sailing in such boats are not harmed by the crocodiles, since these creatures in their own way show either their fear or their reverence for the goddess. The traditional result of Osiris's dismemberment is that there are many so-called tombs of Osiris in Egypt; for Isis held a funeral for each part when she had found it.[6]

Reenactments of Isis's Love for Osiris

The love that Isis showed for her husband, Osiris, and the manner in which that love drove her to resurrect him from the dead had powerful effects on ancient Egyptian society. Not only did those events spawn the most famous of all Egyptian myths—the Myth of Kingship—they also gave average Egyptians hope that they too might experience eternal life after death. So inspiring was this belief among the Egyptians that they instituted an annual celebration of the resurrection myth.

Each year, they presented an elaborate stage play during a religious festival held in the town of Edfu, in southern Egypt. It dramatized not only Osiris's conquest of death but also reenacted how Isis's and Osiris's son Horus fought and defeated Seth for his crime of killing Osiris. According to noted British Museum scholar George Hart, Seth was portrayed as an evil hippopotamus, and the actor playing Horus hunted the creature. "Certainly a model hippopotamus would have been manufactured for the festival," Hart explains. In surviving carvings showing the drama, he goes on, "the symbol of the triumph of Horus is the depiction of him riding the back of the Seth-hippopotamus and spearing its head."

George Hart, *Egyptian Myths*. London: British Museum, 1990, p. 38.

Clearly, Seth had underestimated how deeply Isis had cared about her husband and her dogged determination to get him back. Indeed, after collecting all his body parts, she proceeded to show that restoring him to life had been her objective all along. Carefully and tenderly, she reassembled all the pieces. Then she used several magic spells and elixirs that caused those fragments to attract one another and fuse back together. Soon, Osiris's eyes opened and his chest heaved as he began breathing again. Happily, he and his wife embraced and made love, in the process creating a child who was destined to become the heroic god Horus.

Good-Natured Hathor

Impressed by both the dire suffering Osiris had undergone and his miraculous transformation, the chief Egyptian god, Ra, requested that Osiris depart the earth and assume a new and important position. Thereafter, the former fertility deity and first Egyptian pharaoh became the stately, powerful ruler of the underworld, the domain of dead souls.

This outcome of the Myth of Kingship, a story that appears to have been introduced in the late 2000s BCE, marked a major change in Egyptian views of death and the afterlife. Prior to that era, the accepted view was that only the pharaoh and the few who attended him enjoyed eternal life after death. It was assumed that all other Egyptians simply rotted away in their graves. After Osiris's resurrection and assumption of control of the underworld, however, it was thought that the bulk of the population, even poor folk, achieved salvation in the form of an afterlife.

In Egyptian eyes it had been Isis's deep-seated love for Osiris that had made universal salvation possible. Hence, for most ancient Egyptians love was a strong, ever-present, and positive force in human life and society. The goddess Hathor embodied this

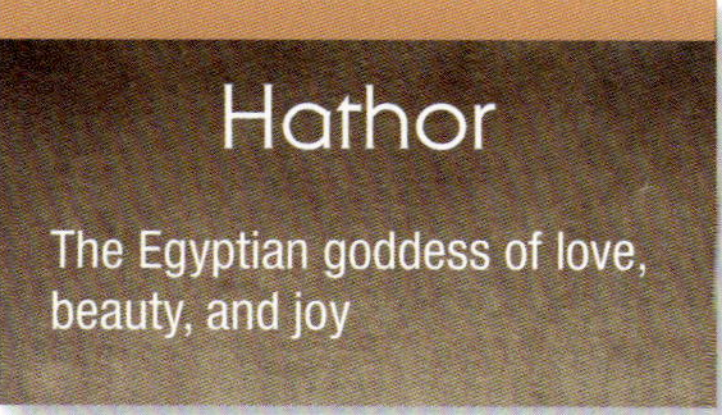

Hathor

The Egyptian goddess of love, beauty, and joy

force. Hathor, a bovine or cow-shaped daughter of Ra, repre-sented love, beauty, and joy.

In spite of being extremely friendly most of the time, however, Hathor did have a temper. She rarely lost it, and not surprisingly, when she did it happened because of the strong love she felt for someone else. The classic case—told in her most famous myth—was when a group of several thousand Egyptians grew unhappy

This gilded image of the head of the cow-shaped love goddess Hathor dates from Egypt's Eighteenth Dynasty, the line of rulers that included the famous pharaoh Tutankhamun (today often called "King Tut"), who ascended the throne in 1336 BCE, more than thirty-three centuries ago.

The Most Detailed Version of the Myth

Various surviving ancient Egyptian writings mention Isis and Osiris, their deep-seated love for each other, and how she brought him back to life after his murder by Seth. By far the primary surviving source for the Myth of Kingship, however, is a work by the first-century-CE Greek writer Plutarch. After becoming a Roman citizen as a young man, he rapidly gained fame as a biographer and essayist, and most of his two largest works have survived. One is the *Parallel Lives*, a collection of fifty biographies of noted Greek and Roman statesmen, military generals, and mythical heroes. The other is the *Moralia*, or "moral essays," made up of dozens of articles that explore the political, religious, mythical, and ethical issues of his time. Among the longer essays in the *Moralia* is one describing the exploits of Isis and Osiris. A veritable treasure chest of information about ancient Egyptian religious traditions and mythology, it is also the most detailed surviving ancient telling of the Myth of Kingship.

with Ra. At the time he was not only their leading god but also the acting ruler of Egypt. A number of these individuals began holding secret meetings in which they plotted to overthrow him in favor of a human king. So Ra held a secret meeting of his own with several other deities, including his daughter Hathor. He told the assembled gods (according to the late Scottish scholar Lewis Spence), "The men whom I have created have conceived evil against me." Then he asked them, "Tell me what shall be done with them?" One of the deities answered, "They shall perish from off the earth!"[7]

Ra felt that completely destroying humanity would be an overreaction. After all, he reasoned, not *all* humans were plotting against him. But in her unbridled love for her father, Hathor lost her temper and attacked the residents of city after city. She likely would have slain every last human. However, some of the other gods intervened on humanity's behalf. They did this because Ra requested it. "I must protect mankind against her," he told those deities (according to a surviving ancient Egyptian writing).

He then ordered them to bring him some mandrake plants. The story continues:

> Straightaway the plants were brought. Now the [gods' human helpers] crushed barley to make beer, and the mandrake plants [which can cause drowsiness when eaten] were added to the mash, and it was [colored] red as human blood. They made seven thousand vases of this beer. Ra came with the gods to look at the beer, and he said, "It is doubly good." And the day broke on which [Hathor] had planned to slaughter [the remnants of] mankind. [And Ra ordered] Let them take the vases of beer to the place where men and women are to be slaughtered.[8]

Just as Ra and the other deities had hoped, Hathor found the containers of beer. Wasting no time, she drank all of the liquid, which made her drunk and sleepy and thereby halted her rampage. When she awoke from a long nap, she went back to being her normal sweet, good-natured self. Her fellow deities all agreed she had shown that love could be the most powerful emotion of all, although not always in a positive way.

CHAPTER TWO

Ancient Greece

In the mythology of the ancient Greeks, the very first god to bring order to a very *dis*ordered universe was Eros. He was the personification of love, and the main Greek creation story says he emerged from a cosmic seed floating in a vast swirling mass of matter called chaos. "From darkness and death," the late, great modern mythologist Edith Hamilton said, "love was born, and with its birth, order and beauty began to banish blind confusion."[9] Eros also brought with him the first rays of light ever seen, the story goes, a divine illumination that shone forth from his magnificent body.

Almost certainly because of Eros's role in the creation of all things, the Greeks came to see him as the god of love. They also recognized a female deity of love—Aphrodite. Not surprisingly, she was the goddess of beauty as well, for in Greek eyes love and beauty were inseparable concepts. That is partly because the Greek myths featured numerous physically beautiful gods and humans. The fact is that, whether rightly or wrongly, the Greeks often equated beauty with goodness and feelings of love and passion. In Hamilton's words:

The world of Greek mythology was not a place of terror for the human spirit. It is true that the gods were disconcertedly incalculable [hard to predict]. One could never tell where Zeus's thunderbolt would strike. Nevertheless, the whole divine company, with a very few and for the most part not important exceptions, were entrancingly beautiful with a human beauty, and nothing humanly beautiful is really terrifying. The early Greek mythologists transformed a world full of fear into a world full of beauty.[10]

Thus, the notion that the Greek myths would contain many stories featuring love—between gods like Aphrodite and Eros, between humans, and between humans and gods—is not surprising.

A Divine Beauty Contest

In fact, Eros and Aphrodite each play roles in multiple myths. The first of Aphrodite's tales depicts her birth from a mass of sea foam that bubbled up after the genitals of an early god named Uranus fell into the sea. Exactly how she sprang into being from that foam remains a mystery. What is more certain is that after the close of the ancient era, many Western artists depicted the event; the most famous version was created in the 1480s by the noted Italian painter Sandro Botticelli. It depicts Aphrodite standing on a giant scallop shell surrounded by images of spring.

One of the first times that Aphrodite's dual role as goddess of both beauty and love came to the fore in a myth was just prior to the start of the famous Trojan War. In that conflict, Paris, a prince of the powerful mercantile city of Troy (located in what is now Turkey) fell in love with Helen, the beautiful wife of Menelaus, ruler of the Greek kingdom of Sparta. The lovers took refuge in Troy, and supposedly that was why an alliance of Greek kings laid siege to that city for a decade.

Helen and Paris did not fall in love merely by chance. Indeed, Aphrodite had much to do with it, as explained in the renowned

Italian artist Sandro Botticelli created this world-famous painting in about 1485. Often called The Birth of Venus *(Venus being the Roman name for the Greek deity Aphrodite), it depicts the love goddess Aphrodite floating up from the sea on a giant clam shell.*

myth frequently called "The Judgment of Paris." Months before traveling to Sparta and meeting its queen, the story goes, Aphrodite had a disagreement with two other deities—Hera, wife of the chief god, Zeus, and Athena, goddess of war and wisdom.

Athena

Goddess of war and wisdom

Each claimed to be the most beautiful of the female divinities, and they argued so heatedly that they almost came to blows. Eventually, they demanded that Zeus referee a contest that would decide which of them was indeed the fairest.

Zeus had no problem with having the contest. But he wisely refrained from being the judge because he knew that no matter which goddess he picked, the other two would never let him hear the end of it. Who could he get to stand in for him, he wondered? At that moment, out of the corner of his eye he noticed young Paris tending some sheep on a mountainside near Troy. The young man was said to be an excellent judge of beauty, Zeus told the three goddesses. The Trojan prince therefore appeared to be a perfect choice to judge the competition.

Not long afterward, Zeus, Aphrodite, Athena, and Hera appeared before the startled Paris and told him he had been chosen for a special job—to determine which of the three goddesses was the most physically stunning. No sooner had the young man accepted the offer than each goddess in her turn tried to bribe him into choosing her. Athera claimed she would make him the leading hero in an upcoming war between the Trojans and Greeks. Hera said she would make him king of both Europe and Asia. Aphrodite promised to make the most beautiful woman in the world fall in love with him.

Did Love Make the World Possible?

According to one of the primary ancient Greek creation myths, the love god Eros emerged from a sort of cosmic seed floating among the jumbled elements making up the disordered early universe. In his play *Birds*, the classical Greek comic playwright Aristophanes described Eros, saying he had "gold wings sprouting from his shoulders." Flapping those wings, he "flew swiftly through the stormy reaches of the swirling cosmos, and embraced it all, in the process mating with it." This brought about an immense burst of light, which illuminated the chaotic spinning substances for the first time. That spectacular act, Aristophanes continued, made possible the appearance of "divine beings, the infinite heavens, the earth, and the oceans' mighty swells."

The early Greek epic poet Hesiod also praised the love god's contributions to the world's creation. Eros was both the embodiment of love, Hesiod wrote, and the "most beautiful of all the deathless gods." This was because there was a special force inhabiting the god's body and mind, a force that over time entered the bodies and minds of all the other gods, as well as those of humans. That special force was the raw, primordial essence of the emotion of love.

Aristophanes, *Birds*, lines 698–702, trans. Don Nardo.

Hesiod, *Theogony*, in Dorothea Wender, trans., *Hesiod and Theognis*. New York: Penguin, 1982, p. 27.

This painting depicts the famous myth in which the Trojan prince Paris chooses Aphrodite as the fairest of the Greek goddesses. This version was created sometime between 1516 and 1528. It is on display in the Fine Arts Museum Basel in Basel, Switzerland.

Being a romantically inclined young man, Paris chose the last option and declared that Aphrodite had won the contest. This was why, during his trip to Sparta, Helen could not resist him and readily ran off with him to Troy. Thus, by judging the contest the way he did, Paris unwittingly contributed to the Greeks' attack on and destruction of his native city.

The Love of Orpheus for Eurydice

One might convincingly argue that the love felt by Paris for Helen and her love for him had been manipulated by the love goddess and therefore was not true love. Assuming that to be the case, Greek mythology does feature several myths that describe very real and pure feelings of love. One of the more outstanding examples is the heartbreaking story of Orpheus and Eurydice.

A brave warrior and skilled musician, Orpheus composed songs that were incredibly moving. In fact, as historians Michael Grant and John Hazel tell it, he "was so marvelous a musician that when he sang and played the lyre [a small harp] the whole of nature would listen entranced, and all creatures would follow him. Even trees and stones were believed to come and hear his music."[11]

Among Orpheus's other fans were young women—both human ones and nymphs (minor nature goddesses). One particularly beautiful and charming nymph, Eurydice, became so enamored of the young man that she could not stop herself from following him almost everywhere he went. Also, without thinking about it, increasingly he directed his loveliest songs at her, and soon he was equally smitten with her. They finally revealed their strong feelings for each other, and it seemed only natural that they should become husband and wife.

The couple enjoyed several years of wedded bliss. Then one day Eurydice was bitten by a poisonous snake. Though nymphs were partly divine, they were not immortal. So the poison eventually killed her. Thus it was that Thanatos, god of death, appeared and led her soul down into the mysterious underworld.

Now alone and overcome with grief, Orpheus pondered what he might do to somehow reverse the situation and get Eurydice back. His friends told him it was useless to think that way. Getting someone back from the underworld, the realm of the powerful god Hades, they advised, was impossible. Now that Eurydice's shade, or soul, had passed on to that subterranean world, it was highly unlikely that Hades would set it free. Yet that is exactly what Orpheus became determined to do. He set his sights on journeying down to Hades's dark kingdom and rescuing his beloved wife.

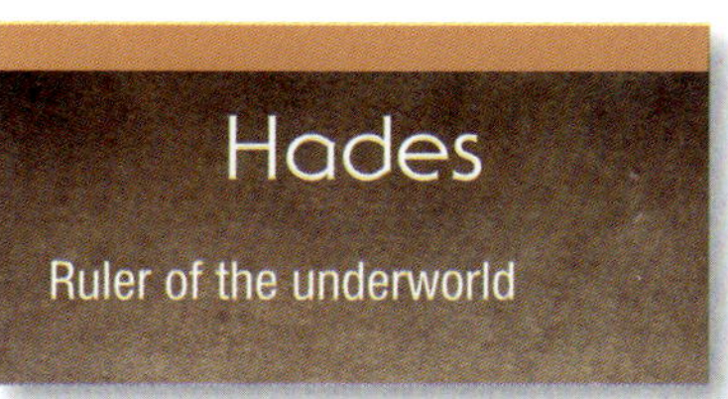

Another Powerful Example of Love

In addition to the love affair between Odysseus and his wife Penelope, Homer's *Odyssey* mentions another powerful example of love—that of Odysseus's dog, Argus, for his master. One of the most moving scenes in all of Greek mythology takes place when Odysseus returns to Ithaca after an absence of twenty years. Before leaving Greece to attack Troy, the man had partially trained Argus, then only a few months old, and the two had become close. During the years his master was away, Argus never forgot him. Remaining loyal, the dog waited patiently, day after day, year after year, for him to come home. Eventually, Argus grew old and the palace servants no longer took proper care of him. When Odysseus finally came back to his palace, he noticed an old hound lying in a pile of donkey manure. In Homer's words, "There lay Argus, covered with flies. Suddenly he heard his master's voice." Happily, "he wagged his tail and dropped his ears. But he no longer had the strength to get up." Fortunately, his eyes still functioned, and "after twenty years of waiting, he looked upon his beloved master." Then faithful Argus leisurely shut his eyes "as death's dark hand closed over him."

Homer, *Odyssey*, Book 17, lines 300–305, 333–335, trans. Don Nardo.

A Mere Millisecond's Mistake

The young man knew that his sword—no matter how skilled he was with it—would be useless against Hades and his supernatural followers. So Orpheus armed himself with what he believed was a much more powerful weapon—his lyre. His plan was to use his music to soften the hearts of those he met in the dimly lit depths and hopefully induce them to free Eurydice. Sure enough, when he encountered Cerberus, the vicious three-headed dog that guarded the underworld's border, he sang and plucked the lyre, and the beast grew quiet and let him pass.

Many hours later, after traversing a maze of dark tunnels deep beneath the earth's surface, Orpheus arrived at Hades's gloomy but impressive palace. To the man's surprise, the lord of the dead was well aware he had arrived and had granted him an audience. Soon

Orpheus stood before Hades, who was dressed in a long black robe, and the queen of the dead, Persephone, who was similarly attired. The man requested that his wife, Eurydice, be released.

Predictably, Hades responded with a firm no. But then the renowned musician started playing his lyre and singing a hauntingly lovely melody. The song was so moving, in fact, that all the grim-looking beings who were guarding the king and queen began weeping. And they were not alone in this reaction. "Even Hades and Persephone were softened," Grant and Hazel write. As a result, "they granted him a favor, allowing him to recover Eurydice on one condition. He must lead the way and not look back at her until they reached the upper air again."[12]

Thrilled at this positive outcome, Orpheus joyfully led his wife upward through the dark tunnels. During the journey, he carefully observed the condition Hades had laid out and refrained from looking back at her. Only a few seconds before they reached the surface, however, he was unable to continue fighting the urge to peek back at Eurydice and did so for a mere millisecond. At that instant, the first-century-BCE Roman poet and mythologist Ovid wrote, the woman suddenly tumbled "back into the depths. Orpheus stretched out his arms, straining to clasp her, but the hapless man touched nothing but yielding air. [Crying out] a last farewell which scarcely reached his ears, she fell back again into the same place from which she had come."[13]

Odysseus and Penelope

Another great ancient Greek love story that involved the intervention of a god was the enduring marriage of Odysseus, ruler of the island kingdom of Ithaca, and his loyal wife and queen, Penelope. Odysseus had been one of the several Greek kings who laid siege to Troy. The cleverest of those rulers, he was the one who introduced the brilliant idea to hide Greek soldiers in a wooden horse and let the Trojans unknowingly drag the object into their city. After ten years of war, he was more than ready to return home to his loving wife. But then his ships were lost at sea, and he wandered through remote regions for another ten years before returning to Ithaca.

After twenty years, Odysseus reasoned, most wives would long since have given up on their absent husbands. But deep down he suspected that Penelope had remained faithful and devoted. And he was right. The problem was that when he returned home, in secret at first, he saw that she was tormented by several dozen young, wealthy suitors, each demanding that she marry him.

No less clever than her husband, Penelope had long kept the suitors at bay through a shrewd trick. Each day she wove threads into a tapestry, saying that when the work was finished she would choose a new mate. But each night she unraveled most of what she had completed that day. This way she was able to keep putting off her decision. Recently, however, the suitors had discovered the ruse and now demanded that she choose one of them within a week.

This illustration shows Odysseus's wife—the ever-loyal Penelope—undoing the tapestry she had worked on earlier that same day. Her strategy was to keep the work unfinished in order to fool the suitors who hounded her.

Odysseus realized that he could not regain his throne and marriage until he had disposed of these intruders in his palace. So he plotted their destruction. Disguised as an old beggar, he revealed himself to his now grown son, Telemachus, and the two, aided by some trusted servants, waited until all the suitors had assembled in the palace banquet hall. Quietly, the true king and the others locked the interlopers inside. Then Odysseus stepped forward, removed his beggar's clothes, and called the suitors yellow dogs. "You never thought to see me back from Troy," he told them. "So you ate me out of house and home; you raped my maids; you wooed my wife [and now] I tell you, one and all, that your doom is sealed."[14]

Realizing they must fight for their lives and filled with fear, the suitors ran back and forth in confusion. But with the doors barred, they were trapped. Some tried to fight back, but the war goddess Athena, who greatly admired Odysseus, intervened and caused their weapons to falter. As a result, one by one, Odysseus, his son, and the servants slaughtered the suitors until the hall's floor was slippery with human blood.

The Triumph of Love

When the battle was over, Odysseus and Penelope were finally able to be reunited. After some official greetings in front of family and invited guests, the two retired to their bedchamber. There rested the wedding bed that Odysseus had long before constructed with his own hands from wood taken from olive trees. Despite so many years apart, they had both remained steadfast and true to each other in a loving union that neither time nor circumstance could shatter. Hugging each other tightly and overwhelmed with feelings of happiness, they felt tears welling up and were reluctant to end the embrace. To extend this tender scene for the lovers, with a wave of her divine hand Athena delayed the coming of the dawn. In the days that followed, the Ithacan people were overjoyed knowing that love had triumphed over adversity.

CHAPTER THREE

Ancient Rome

In the annals of Roman mythology, no one either venerated or indulged in the affairs of love more than Venus. This was hardly surprising, since after all, she was the Roman goddess of love. Indeed, the largely conservative and at times prudish Romans would have labeled a human woman with many lovers promiscuous and untrustworthy. But in judging Venus's many romantic affairs, the general consensus was that she could be forgiven, since powerful attractions for the opposite sex were simply part of her nature. And in any case she was a goddess, so it was not humans' place to judge her anyway.

Moreover, all Romans agreed that, promiscuous or not, Venus was a vital link in the ancestry of the Roman people, and for that reason she must be respected. The tale of how that connection between the love goddess and the Roman people came about began when she suddenly and unexpectedly arose from the depths of the sea. Soon afterward, she joined the company of the other gods, led by mighty Jupiter. The latter urged her to marry his son, Vulcan, the gods' blacksmith and the deity of fire.

The problem with that union was that both parties tended to cheat on their mates. Vulcan produced at least four offspring with other women, divine and mortal alike. At the same time, Venus grew bored with her forge-working husband and had affairs with other gods.

The most intense of those relationships was with another of Jupiter's sons, Mars, god of war. Venus and Mars proceeded to have five children together, among them Cupid, a love deity who was renowned for shooting arrows that made the people they struck fall in love.

Venus had love affairs with mortal men, too. One was a Trojan named Anchises, and the product of that union was Aeneas, at first a Trojan prince and later the founder of the Roman race. The second-century-CE Roman writer now called Pseudo-Hyginus wrote that Venus "loved Anchises and [lay] with him. By him she conceived Aeneas, but she warned him not to reveal it to anyone. Anchises, however, told it [while drinking] wine with his companions, and for this was struck by the thunderbolt of Jove [Jupiter]."[15]

The importance of Venus's and Anchises's love for each other becomes evident when one realizes that their grandson—Aeneas's son Ascanius—later founded the Italian community that over time developed into Rome. That made Venus in a very real sense the great-, great-, and many more times great-grandmother of the Roman people.

Love in Carthage

Today it is well known that many, if not most, of the stories in Roman mythology were borrowed from the Greeks. The Romans conquered the Greek lands in the last few centuries BCE and, struck by the greatness of Greek art and literature, absorbed much of it. In the process, the Romans came to associate many of their own deities with more impressive Greek ones. (Venus, for instance, was the Roman version of the Greek love goddess Aphrodite.)

Nevertheless, the Romans eventually developed some original myths of their own, often adding to or reinventing older Greek tales. That was how Aeneas, in Greek mythology strictly

Cupid (the Roman version of the Greek love god Eros) binds two Roman deities—Venus, goddess of love, and Mars, god of war—with the aim of keeping them forever united in love. This painting depicting the myth was created in the 1570s.

a Trojan prince, became the founder of the Roman race in Roman mythology. In particular, this crucial story was the work of the first-century-BCE Roman poet and mythologist Virgil. His magnificent epic the *Aeneid*, which instantly became the Romans' proud national epic, describes how Aeneas, carrying old Anchises on his back, escaped the burning Troy. Subsequently, guided and urged on by his mother, Venus, Aeneas made it to Italy and established the family line that would later lead to Romulus, founder of Rome.

Considering that the mythological love affair between Venus and Anchises had set the grandiose plot of Rome's chief national myth in motion, it is not surprising that Virgil made love a major theme of that tale. One of the other powerful love affairs that unfolds during Aeneas's journey to Italy takes place in Carthage (in what is now Tunisia, in North Africa). There, the former Trojan prince enjoyed a splendid feast with that kingdom's queen, Dido, and her nobles. "Come, dear guest," she said to Aeneas, "tell us the whole tale from the beginning, [including] the cunning of the Greeks, your country's ruin, and your wanderings."[16]

After Aeneas told his story in detail, he met with Queen Dido a few other times, and during those interactions she fell deeply in love with him. Thus, she did not want him to sail on to Italy but pleaded with him to stay with her in Carthage. This upset Venus, who was adamant that her son establish the Roman lineage. So she complained to Jupiter, who sent his messenger, Mercury, to

Driven by Divine Prophecies

The strong will of the love goddess Venus was not the only factor that drove Aeneas to make his way to Italy. Also, multiple gods delivered prophecies that foretold the rise of Rome and the part he was fated to play in it. One such prediction was made by the Greco-Roman god of prophecy himself, Apollo. Immediately following Troy's fall, he proclaimed, "There is a place the Greeks have called Hesperia, the western land." The people who live there, he said, call themselves "Italians, after Italus, one of their leaders. There lies [Aeneas's] true home." That prophecy persuaded the Trojan prince that he should make his way to Italy. Later, when he made it there, he encountered the Sibyl, a mysterious woman wearing a black robe. Rumors suggested that she could foresee and predict future events. Sure enough, she entered into a trance and informed Aeneas that he would help establish a new kingdom in west-central Italy. The Sibyl also led Aeneas down into the dark underworld, where he found the ghost of his father, Anchises. "Our glorious Rome," the old man said, "shall rule the whole wide world, and her spirit shall match the spirit of the gods."

Virgil, *Aeneid*, trans. Patric Dickinson. New York: New American Library, 2002, pp. 67, 172–73.

speak with Aeneas. "What are you doing?" Mercury asked Aeneas. "Why do you linger here in North Africa?"[17] The god then persuaded him to continue his all-important voyage to Italy.

When Dido heard this, she was livid and shouted at Aeneas, saying, "You traitor! Did you hope to mask such treachery and silently slink from my land?"[18] There was nothing to be done, however. Aeneas did love Dido and did not deny it, but in his mind his divinely driven quest across the storm-tossed Mediterranean Sea took precedence over his personal romantic desires.

Love Among the Romans and Sabines

Still another story of romance from the larger tale of Aeneas's adventures consisted of his later falling in love with and marrying an Italian princess. Venus, who still kept an eye on her son's exploits, was suspected of instigating romantic feelings in the couple.

Moreover, that goddess was far from finished with ensuring that her beloved Rome, which Jupiter had prophesied would eventually arise in Italy, would grow successful and powerful. Several generations after Aeneas and his wife passed on, she felt it was time to once again intervene in earthly affairs.

This time it was shortly after an ambitious young descendant of Aeneas—Romulus—had officially established the town of Rome, on seven low hills near the Tiber River, in western Italy. At first he had only about one hundred followers, clearly not enough to create a large city. So to "fill up his big new town," the first-century-BCE Roman historian Livy wrote, Romulus made it "a place of asylum for fugitives. Here fled for refuge all the [outcasts] from the neighboring peoples, some free, some slaves, and all of them wanting nothing more than a fresh start."[19]

Although Rome's population did quickly grow, the problem was that almost all of the new arrivals were men. Romulus was at first stumped about what to do. But his divine overseer, Venus, looking down from above, knew exactly what needed to be done. She quietly implanted in him the idea that the infant Romans required a potent infusion of romantic love. Indeed, the growing numbers of male Romans needed to have wives they could love and trust and with whom they could have children. Some of these offspring would of course be female, and in that way Roman society would begin to produce its own native women. Venus could be counted on to imbue those women with feelings of love for their husbands, and thereby the future expansion of Roman society would be assured. A healthy mix of marriage and romantic love, Romulus suddenly decided, might well make Rome an unstoppable force in the world.

To that end, Rome's founder hatched a bold plan. He sent word to the residents of all the nearby towns that the Romans were going to have a large-scale religious holiday and festival. There would be food, entertainment, and athletic contests for all. Many of those who attended were unmarried female members of a Latin-speaking people known as the Sabines. In the midst of the celebration, at Romulus's signal, hundreds of male Romans confronted and made passes at those women, in some cases demanding the women marry them.

Romulus sent messengers to the Sabine towns and assured their leaders that the women were being well treated. The women would be married, he said, and enjoy "all the privileges of the community," according to Livy, "and they would be bound to their husbands by the dearest bond of all—[love for] their children."[20]

But the Sabine leaders were too angry to listen. They sent an army, which marched right into Rome's heart. Decked out in heavy metal armor, soldiers on both sides were about to clash when something very unexpected occurred. The Sabine women charged out onto the battlefield and stood between the opposing armies. They implored the fighters to lay down their weapons. Having fallen in love with their Roman husbands, they said, they desired that the two peoples come together and live in peace. The power of love had won the day, and Rome subsequently became greater as a result.

The Angry Goddess

Venus, along with her son, the love god Cupid, had roles in other Roman myths as well, including what many modern scholars view as one of the two or three greatest love stories in all of world mythology. An early version of it was told by the Greeks. But by far the most detailed and famous version was that of the second-century-CE Roman novelist Apuleius. It begins in an unnamed ancient kingdom located somewhere in northern Italy. The king and queen of that realm had three beautiful daughters, the youngest of whom, Psyche, was the most lovely of all. In fact, she was so physically stunning that many of the locals came to see her as worthy of worship. Of those people, several actually neglected their usual worship of the love deity Venus so that they could bow down before Psyche as she walked by them in the streets.

When Venus discovered what was happening, she "could not control her irritation," in Apuleius's words. "She tossed her head,

This painting from 1895 shows the famous lovers Cupid and Psyche. Each fell deeply in love with the other, despite Venus's fervent desire to destroy the young woman. Eventually, Jupiter gave Psyche the gift of immortality.

let out a deep growl, and spoke to herself: 'Here am I, the ancient mother of the universe . . . compelled to share the glory of my majesty with a mortal maiden!'"[21] At that moment the goddess vowed to make Psyche pay for her insolence. To that end, Venus demanded that her incredibly handsome son, Cupid, make the young woman fall deeply in love with the most disgusting man in the world. That way, the goddess hoped, Psyche would waste her life and be miserable.

Psyche's First Sight of Cupid

The Roman writer Apuleius's well-written novel *The Golden Ass* contains a particularly beautiful passage describing Psyche's first glimpse of her mysterious lover and husband, who turns out to be the love god Cupid. "As soon as the [oil] lamp was brought near," it reads in part,

> she beheld of all beasts the gentlest and sweetest, Cupid himself, a handsome god lying in a handsome posture. Even the lamplight was cheered and brightened on sighting him. . . . As for Psyche, she was awe-struck at this wonderful vision, and she lost all of her self-control. She swooned and paled . . . [and] her knees buckled. . . . She gazed down on him in distraction, and as she passionately smothered him with wanton kisses from parted lips, she feared that he might stir in his sleep. But while her wounded heart pounded on being roused by such striking beauty, the lamp disgorged a drop of burning oil from the tip of its flame upon the god's right shoulder. . . . The god started up on being burnt; he saw that he was exposed [to her sight], and that his trust was defiled [betrayed].

Apuleius, *The Golden Ass*, trans. P.G. Walsh. New York: Oxford University Press, 1995, pp. 92–93.

A Voice in the Dark

Cupid initially planned to obey his mother. But then he secretly caught sight of Psyche and instantly fell in love with her. Behind Venus's back, he used his divine powers to cause Psyche to travel alone to a deserted valley. There, she caught sight of a small but splendid-looking palace. Entering, she saw that it was beautifully decorated. Then she heard a pleasant voice say, "All these things are yours." The voice added, "Once you have completed freshening up, a royal feast will at once be laid before you."[22]

Later that night, Psyche felt a man crawl into bed with her, but it was too dark in the room to allow her to identify him. Yet for reasons she could not then explain, she trusted him, and over the weeks that followed the two developed a truly loving relation-ship. They even married, although she still had not seen what he looked like. He insisted that it must remain so forever. But eventu-ally she could stand the mystery no longer. Determined to see her husband in the flesh, one night she crept into a dark room where he was sleeping. With the aid of an oil lamp, she finally gazed on him and saw the magnificence of his physical form.

Cupid suddenly awakened and accused his young wife of be-traying his trust. He abruptly vanished, and she became determined to search for as long as it might take to find him and win back his trust. However, Venus had recently learned that her son had wooed and married Psyche, and to gain revenge she forced the maiden into a deep, coma-like sleep. That might have been the girl's end. Luck-ily for her, however, Cupid found out what had happened, rushed to her side, and used his considerable powers to awaken her.

Everlasting Love

Then Cupid brought his young wife before mighty Jupiter, who proclaimed that the lovers must henceforth be free from harm and allowed to partake of their love in peace. The chief god also convinced Venus to quench her hatred for her new daughter-in-law. Finally, Jupiter gave Psyche the gift of immortality so that she could always remain at Cupid's side. In this way, the powerful bond between the god of love and Psyche, whose name means "the soul," became imperishable and everlasting.

CHAPTER FOUR

Ancient India

The Hindus of ancient India had numerous myths related to love and lovers. Of those, one of the most often told and retold was the story of how the heroic doctor Yama Kumar outwitted the god of death. What adds extra drama to the tale is the fact that Yama Kumar was the son of that widely feared deity—Yama. The latter had years before married a mortal woman, who gave birth to a son they named Yama Kumar. As the boy grew older, he became fascinated with various medicinal herbs, and in time that interest led him to study medicine. By the time he was in his mid-twenties he was one of the best-known physicians in India.

Around that same time Yama Kumar heard the news that a young princess in a nearby kingdom had become gravely ill. Moreover, the word was that her court physicians were stumped on how to cure her. A kind, caring individual, Yama Kumar decided to see what he could do to help the princess, and a few days later he arrived in the realm ruled by her father. That king was grateful that the young man had made the journey and led him to the young woman's bedchamber.

As they entered the room, Yama Kumar was immediately disturbed by what he saw. His own father—the deity of death—was standing beside the princess's bed. In the words of modern Indian myth teller Sowmya Rajendran, Yama Kumar "begged and pleaded with Yama to leave the room. But the god of death said sadly, 'Her time has come, son. Since you are pleading with me so much, I will leave her for three days. But after that her life belongs to me.'"[23]

In the days that followed, the young doctor declined to leave the princess's bedside and tried nearly every medical treatment he knew. None of them were successful, however. In the meantime, the sight of his patient, who retained her considerable beauty even on her deathbed, caused him to fall in love with her, which gave him added motivation to heal her.

The problem was that time rapidly ran out. As Yama Kumar feared, at the end of the third day his stern-looking father, Yama, arrived, bent on collecting the dying princess's soul. At that instant, Yama Kumar tried a desperate ploy in a last-ditch effort to save the young woman he hoped eventually to marry. He lied

A bronze statuette, dating from the 1700s, shows the Hindu god of death, Yama. His son, Yama Kumar, became a leading Indian physician who sought to help a young princess who was dying. By saving her, the young man kept her from his own father's clutches.

to his father, saying that a minor deity whom Yama hated with a passion was in the adjoining room and would be helping the god of death harvest the girl's soul. Seriously desiring to avoid seeing that fellow deity, Yama told his son he would return in a week or two and hurriedly departed.

This was the opening that Yama Kumar had hoped for. Having a little more time to try a few more potential cures, he finally managed to put the princess on the road to recovery. In less than a week, she was almost back to her normal self, which meant that the god of death no longer had a reason to visit her. Furthermore, in time she and Yama Kumar became husband and wife, with the blessing of that realm's heartily appreciative ruler and many subjects.

The Sun God's Wife

To countless Hindus over the centuries, the main message of Yama Kumar's myth has been that in certain circumstances true love has the power to overcome death. In fact, love and its rewards are a frequent theme of Hindu mythology and literature. There are an "amazing variety of mythical love stories" from ancient India, says popular Indian writer Subhamoy Das. They make up one of the world's "richest treasure hoards of exciting love tales,"[24] he adds.

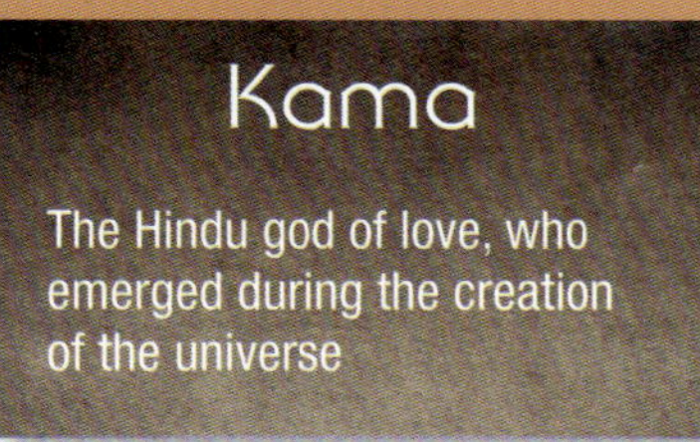
Kama

The Hindu god of love, who emerged during the creation of the universe

Some of those delightful stories feature the Hindu god of love and desire, Kama, and his mate, the love goddess Rati. In contrast, other ancient Indian myths about love contain other characters who are at least inspired or motivated by those love deities. What makes these myths unusual is their sheer number, arguably more than in any other national mythology with the exception of that of the Greeks. Modern Indian myth teller Kavita Kane points out that "the proliferation of romantic themes [in Indian mythology] is not necessarily as tragic as [it]

In the powerful story of the lovers Heer and Ranjha, sometimes called the "Hindu Romeo and Juliet," Ranjha was a carefree young man. After his father died and his older brothers unfairly denied him any of the family inheritance, he began traveling and eventually reached the small city of Jhang. There he took a job on a local farm and soon met his boss's daughter, the beautiful Heer. Ranjha and Heer fell deeply in love. But when Heer's father found out, he forbade her from seeing Ranjha, believing the young man to be unworthy of his daughter. To keep the lovers apart, the father arranged for the young woman to marry a local landowner. Ranjha eventually found out where Heer's new husband was keeping her under lock and key and hurried to the house. There he managed to break her free, and the two escaped. They went to a high government official, who took their side in the case, and they were allowed to remain together. However, Heer's spiteful parents sent a basket of poisoned candy to the couple, and Heer ate some and died. Ranjha then purposely ate some of the candy and died while holding his beloved's body.

was in Greek mythology, [yet] is astounding in its sheer depth and diversity. Love was honored and revealed [in Indian society] as a powerful emotion and . . . love [is portrayed as] vital to the scheme of existence."[25]

Thus, the depictions of romantic love in the ancient Hindu myths mirror the complications and importance of love in real life. And nowhere in the old Indian tales is that complexity illustrated more clearly than in the myth of Surya and his lover Sanjana. Surya was the deity of the sun, and as a result his face was so blindingly bright that no one could look directly at him. Sanjana was the daughter of another god, Vishvakarman, who inspired creative abilities in humans. Vishvakarman wanted his daughter to marry a fellow deity, which is why he made a deal with Surya, who agreed to wed her.

At first, Sanjana was reluctant because she did not like the idea of an arranged

Vishvakarman

The Hindu deity who is thought to inspire creative abilities in human beings

The Hindu sun god Surya appears in a number of myths, including the one in which he falls in love with Sanjana, the daughter of another deity. This sumptuous image of the radiant Surya hangs in the palace of the ancient and medieval rulers of Mewar, a region in northwestern India.

marriage in which love played no part. However, as time went by, she discovered that Surya was actually smart, friendly, and fun to talk to. Little by little she fell in love with him. One obstacle to the relationship was the fact that she could never look directly at him because of his blindingly bright face. However, she learned to close her eyes tightly when they embraced, and that way they were able to have children. First came a son, whom they named Manu, and later they had twins, a girl and a boy.

Not long after the twins arrived, for reasons that no one knows, Surya's mood changed. He came to suspect that his wife was tired of squinting and closing her eyes when they were together.

She denied that was the case, but he became convinced of it and lost his temper and yelled at her.

Sanjana was crestfallen. She did not want to leave her husband, but his mood change made her feel increasingly unhappy. So eventually she decided to try a novel approach. Because she was the offspring of a god, she had certain latent powers. One of these was the ability to project an image of herself in the form of a woman who looked and sounded exactly like her. She gave this image the name Chhaya, meaning "shadow."

Life and Love in the Forest

Sanjana proceeded to train Chhaya in how to impersonate her, and the shadow woman took over the real wife's position in the house. Surya had no idea he was now living with a shadow wife instead of the real Sanjana. In the meantime, the actual Sanjana slipped away into a vast forest and made herself look like a horse. In that disguise, she reasoned, her husband would be unlikely ever to find her.

The scheme might well have worked had Chhaya been a perfect copy of Sanjana. But the reality was that looks and actions were not enough. Chhaya lacked Sanjana's emotional qualities, especially her ability to love her husband and children and to show that love. After a while, Surya noticed that the woman he thought was his wife often neglected the children and treated them in a cold manner. In fact, at one point Manu came to him and said, "Father, this lady who is so unkind to us cannot be our mother! She is someone else, I am sure!"[26] As a result, Surya became convinced that this woman was indeed an imposter. Hence, the sun god finally cornered Chhaya and forced her to tell the truth.

It was now Surya's turn to be crestfallen. He truly loved his wife and now set out to find her. It took several months of searching, but he eventually heard a rumor that she was in the forest and had taken a horse's form. Hurrying into the woods, he wisely made himself look equine, which had an unusual side effect.

Namely, it significantly reduced his level of brightness, so that he no longer blinded those who looked at him. Only a few hours after he underwent that transformation, he spotted a beautiful female horse in a clearing and immediately knew it was Sanjana. The two were reunited, and she was overjoyed that for the first time ever she could look directly at her husband. They decided to remain in the forest, living as horses, for at least a few more years. The children visited them there sometimes, and the rest of the time they were supervised by Chhaya, who came to love them nearly as much as their parents did.

Krishna: Lover and Prankster

The feelings of love that drove Surya and Sanjana to reunite and overcome the complexities of their life together were strong. But an overview of love and lovers in world mythology reveals that no one—whether divine or human—tried harder to live for love than the Hindu god Vishnu. He bore the popular nickname of the Preserver because, out of his love for life and nature, he worked tirelessly to protect and maintain the universe's physical structure. To accomplish that lofty goal, he sometimes took on disguises, or avatars, in which he assumed alternate personalities.

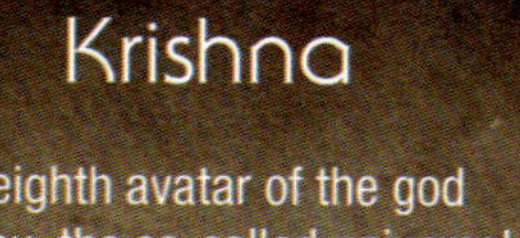

The eighth avatar of the god Vishnu, the so-called universal protector

All of those avatars were admirable and heroic in one way or another. But among them the most lovable and playful was Vishnu's eighth incarnation—Krishna. He grew up herding cattle in Gokul, a town in northern India, and initially neither his parents nor his acquaintances in the area realized he was a divine being. At the time, that region was home to far more women than men, and by chance when Krishna was young, he was the only male youth in Gokul. That fact, combined with his phenomenal good looks, made him a sensation among the local female cowherds, called *gopis*.

Love the Guiding Force in Nature?

Kama, the Hindu god of love, has much in common with the Greek god of love, Eros. In fact, the Hindu myth in which Kama is instrumental to the emergence of the visible universe and life within it is almost identical in several ways to the Greek myth describing Eros's role in the creation. In both stories the cosmos is initially utterly dark, formless, and devoid of life. In the Greek version, Eros appears from a cosmic seed, and in the Hindu version Kama comes from a "seed of the mind." Both gods are described as the motivation for all life, implying that the desire known as love is the guiding force in nature. The ancient Hindu text known as the *Rig Veda* says about Kama's emergence, "In the beginning, darkness was hidden by darkness with no distinguishing sign. . . . The life force that was covered with emptiness arose through the power of heat. Desire (Kama) arose in it in the beginning. That was the first seed of the mind. Wise sages seeking in their hearts, with wisdom, found it to be the bond that connects existence with non-existence."

Quoted in Sunita Shah, "Kamadeva the God of Love," *The Jai Jais* (blog), December 13, 2020. https://thejaijais.com.

Almost every gopi hoped for the honor of being Krishna's girlfriend—and eventually his wife. That was why they all went along with the various harmless and usually charming pranks he played on them. In one of the most memorable, which is to this day told and retold in India, he took their clothes while they were swimming naked in a pond. In order to recover those garments, each gopi had to walk from the water to where Krishna stood holding the clothes. He told them not to worry because he would keep his eyes shut, but considering his playful nature, it is unlikely that he kept that promise.

Another way that Krishna and the young cowgirls interacted was to attend local dances sponsored by the town elders. He did not want to hurt anyone's feelings, so he avoided playing favorites among the girls. Near the start of a dance, therefore, he rapidly grew several extra arms of differing lengths; that way he was able to dance with all of the gopis simultaneously.

The Highest Form of Love

The time came, however, when Krishna fell madly in love with a gopi named Radha. The other cowgirls were disappointed at not being chosen, but they all greatly admired both Radha and

Krishna. So they sincerely wished the two lovers well and even sometimes acted as their bodyguards.

Later, Krishna employed his divine powers to cause Radha's soul to fly out of her mortal body. That spirit of hers floated directly to him and joined with his own, forming a unique heavenly union. That sacred merger is, in the eyes of Hindus in each succeeding generation, the crucial and serious outcome of a myth that began with idle playfulness. The belief is that a pure and holy kind of love exists, as exemplified by Krishna and Radha. As explained in the popular Hindu website Magik India, "The relationship between Krishna and the gopis is not a sexual one, but rather the feeling of the highest love. Krishna was not a 'playboy,' but the incarnation of pure love. [Hence] the devotion and unconditional love of Radha for Krishna can be seen as the symbol of the soul longing from the divine and merging with it. It is the unique relationship between mankind and God."[27]

Ancient China

Throughout most of China's long history, people have frequently described the moon as sad and lonely. Night after night, year after year, and century after century, the story goes, it pines away for a love it lost long ago. One of several Chinese myths about love and lovers, this one features the moon goddess, Chang'e, and the legendary expert archer Hou Yi.

The story starts in the dimly remembered past when the world was still fairly young, an antique era in which ten suns loomed in the sky. Because of this overabundance of suns, it was very hot and humid on the earth, and night did not yet exist. All that excess heat made a majority of farmers' crops wither, and as a result there were intermittent periods of starvation among humans.

One of those individuals, the brave archer Hou Yi, finally decided that this destructive situation must end. Collecting his weapons, he went to a wide meadow, raised his trusty bow, and one by one shot down nine of the ten suns. Afterward, the nature goddess Xiwangmu congratulated and praised the man, saying he had done humans and gods alike a major service. As a reward, she gave him a vial containing the so-called elixir of immortality, a liquid that made any human who drank it an immortal deity.

Hou Yi went home to his wife, Chang'e, whom he loved dearly, and told her what had happened. The goddess had given him enough of the elixir for only one person, he explained. And because of his deep love for his wife, he had decided not to drink it because it would mean leaving her behind to age and die. Chang'e was grateful because she loved her husband no less than he loved her. But that night, after he fell asleep, she had a moment of weakness. She drank the elixir and soon began to exhibit divine traits. She floated upward into the sky, and not long afterward, with Hou Yi looking on in horror, she transformed into the moon.

The man mourned his lost wife, and in similar fashion she regretted parting from him. Her sadness grew when she learned that her action could not be reversed or undone. Forever after she remained lonely and sad for the loss of true love.

In this illustration of a famous ancient Chinese myth, the woman Chang'e is about to drink the magic elixir that will transform her into the moon goddess. The story of her conversion from a mortal into an immortal is widely seen in China as a sad tale of lost love and loneliness.

The Herder and the Cloud Weaver

An important side story to the myth of Chang'e is the manner in which ancient Chinese society incorporated it into a real-life cultural tradition. It takes the form of a special celebration based on what Hou Yi supposedly did after losing his beloved spouse. Hoping to make her feel less lonely, the tale goes, once each year for the rest of his life he left samples of her favorite desserts and fruits out in an open field, in case she might somehow consume them. Over time the tradition continued and steadily developed into the annual Mid-Autumn Festival. That celebration "is a special time where people can reflect on the past year with family, friends, and food,"[28] modern journalist and myth teller Mae Hamilton explains.

Modern experts are unsure about exactly when the myth and the festival based on it emerged. What is more certain is that

Hou Yi

The legendary ancient archer who shot down nine of the original ten suns

These so-called "moon cakes" are widely popular in China, particularly during the annual Mid-Autumn Festival. Originally, it celebrated the small desserts that the husband of Chang'e left out for her after she was transformed. Today it is seen mainly as a day for friendly family get-togethers.

A Holiday Based on a Popular Myth

Among China's most popular cultural holidays, the Mid-Autumn Festival is based largely on the famous myth of Chang'e and how she became the goddess of the moon after swiping the elixir of immortality and drinking it. Another reason the festival developed was to celebrate yearly harvests of food staples, especially rice and wheat. Most often the holiday is observed by members of families, along with friends and coworkers. It is leisurely and features a congenial, good-time atmosphere in which people get together, share meals and drinks, and reminisce about positive memories of the past. It is also common for the celebrants to place candy, fruits, desserts, and other tasty treats on open-air altars dedicated to Chang'e. It is thought that she appreciates these offerings and, if satisfied, blesses those who gave them. In addition, some people bake mooncakes (made from red beans and lotus seeds) and decorate them with images of the goddess or her pet rabbit.

Chinese culture itself first arose in the mid- to late 2000s BCE along the banks of the Yellow River, in northeastern China. Some myths, including some about love and lovers, likely existed in that early period. But because they were passed along by word of mouth rather than written down, it is not possible to determine which myths initially existed and when they appeared.

It was not until close to two millennia later, in the last few centuries BCE, that the Chinese began to record their myths in writing. By that time, a very large and rich collection of those ancient tales had developed, several of which featured the theme of love and its importance to the human condition. Among them was one that remains a favorite today in China among people of all ages and walks of life—the story of Niu Lang and Zhi Nu.

Long ago when the universe was young, the story goes, the brightest stars in the sky were inhabited by semidivine beings similar to the angels envisioned by Christianity. Niu Lang was the essence of the masculine star Altair, and Zhi Nu occupied the feminine star Vega. The two got to know each other and fell in love. However, they had to keep those feelings secret because Xiwangmu, who as nature goddess also controlled the sky, frowned on such romances.

Unfortunately for the two, Xiwangmu discovered their relationship and decided to punish them. Because Zhi Nu was one of the goddess's granddaughters, she went easy on her. The former manifestation of Vega now became a cloud weaver, a minor nature spirit who fashioned clouds into pretty patterns in the sky. Niu Lang, meanwhile, was demoted to the lowly position of a human cowherd in an earth village.

The Cow's Secret

The two former lovers were miserable about being separated. Zhi Nu cried every single day. Niu Lang never smiled, and both secretly daydreamed about seeing each other again someday. Those dreams eventually came true. Many years after the two had parted company, Xiwangmu allowed her granddaughters, including Zhi Nu, to visit the earth and bathe in a pond in the lush park known as the Lotus Garden.

By this time Niu Lang had fallen into poverty and despair. His only possessions were an aging cow, which became his only friend, and a rickety wooden cart. The young herder managed to construct a small, crude shack, and he and the cow lived there together, often not seeing anyone else for months at a time. Then one day the cow said to Niu Lang, "Today you shall go to the Lotus Garden. There you will see angels bathing. You must find the robes that are red in color and you must steal them and hide them." Why must this be done? asked Niu Lang. The cow's answer was, "The red robes are the robes that belong to the one who will be your wife."[29]

This information intrigued the herder, so he did as the cow suggested and made his way to the Lotus Garden. Hiding in the grass, he watched the so-called angels arrive and saw that they were wearing attractive red robes. After the young women

removed the garments and entered the pond, Niu Lang did as the cow had instructed and collected the robes. He was about to hide them when the bathers saw him. They took back their clothes and swiftly donned them, then all but one of them flew upward toward the sky. The one who stayed was none other than Zhi Nu, although Niu Lang did not recognize her at this point. But she recognized him, and that was why she did not flee. In the minutes that followed, she revealed her identity, and the two fell into each other's arms.

Filled with joy at having found each other again, Zhi Nu and Niu Lang married. After that, for many years they dwelled in the small house he had built with his own hands, and in time they had two children. Zhi Nu weaved cotton and made clothes, and Niu Lang raised crops with the help of his faithful friend, the cow.

One day the cow died. But just before closing its eyes for the last time, it told Niu Lang a secret it had long been keeping. The secret was that the cow had once been a series of stars in the sky, too. It had been the famous Taurus, the bull. Xiwangmu had grown angry with it and had punished it by transforming it into an earthly cow. But while on earth it had chosen to look after its former fellow star spirits—Niu Lang and Zhi Nu—the best it could.

China's Romeo and Juliet

Eventually, according to this myth, Niu Lang and Zhi Nu returned to the sky and became stars again. Meanwhile, on earth, as Chinese civilization continued to develop, the story of those lovers remained and grew increasingly popular. A special day was set aside each year to remember and honor them. Still celebrated today, it is often referred to as the Chinese Valentine's Day.

Another Chinese myth about heartfelt love has been given a nickname in Western countries as well. Frequently called the "Chinese Romeo and Juliet," its main characters are Liang Shanbo and Zhu Yingtai, together better known in China as the Butterfly Lovers. Zhu Yingtai, usually called simply Zhu for short, started life as the exceedingly smart but brash and spoiled young daughter of a rich Chinese government administrator. In this early Chinese era, females did not go to school. School was a privilege reserved for well-to-do boys. But Zhu refused to follow social tradition. She secretly snuck out of her family's house and enrolled in school disguised as a young man. Each afternoon, she returned home and changed back into her female clothing, so her parents were none the wiser.

When Zhu began going to her classes, one young man immediately caught her attention. His name was Liang Shanbo. The two were instantly attracted to each other, and within a week they were best friends. "For three years, they studied hard together," one modern myth teller writes. "All the while, Zhu was careful never to reveal her true identity, and Liang Shanbo did not discover her secret."[30]

The Defeat of Death

When the three years were up, Zhu found out to her dismay that her father had arranged for her to marry a man she barely knew and definitely did not love. Realizing she needed to devote all of her time to halting the marriage, the young woman abruptly stopped attending classes. Liang was at a loss to understand what had happened to his closest friend, so one day after classes he went to the large house where Zhu's family dwelled. When he asked to see the family's son, a servant told him there was no such person. He was further surprised to learn that the family only had a daughter. In this way, Liang discovered the truth about Zhu's gender.

Liang understood why Zhu had pretended to be a young man. When he found out what was going on, he boldly approached her parents and asked for her hand in marriage. Because he came from a family with little money, they rudely rejected him. Thinking all was lost, he died of grief. When Zhu heard about Liang's untimely passing, she herself lost the will to live. Running to his grave site, she saw that his wooden coffin had not yet been buried, and without hesitation she climbed into it.

A few minutes later, Zhu's distraught parents and other relatives caught up, and as they approached the coffin they beheld something unexpected and strange. From a crack in the container's lid there emerged a pair of lovely butterflies, which fluttered around and then disappeared across a nearby sunlit meadow. Even stranger was the fact that when Zhu's parents opened the coffin, they found it was empty.

In the years that followed, a legend grew about the tragic young couple. So great was their love, that story claimed, that it touched the hearts of the gods, who could not bear to see Zhu and Liang separated forever. And so, some divinities whose names were never revealed intervened and allowed true love to defeat cruel and solitary death.

Introduction: Timeless, Universal Tales of Love

1. Ferdowsi, *The Epic of Kings*, trans. Helen Zimmern, Internet Classics Archive. http://classics.mit.edu.
2. Ferdowsi, *The Epic of Kings*.
3. Alia El Saady, "Myths and Legends of Love," Identity, February 6, 2017. https://identity-mag.com.

Chapter One: Ancient Egypt

4. Apuleius, *The Golden Ass*, trans. P.G. Walsh. New York: Oxford University Press, 1995, pp. 219–20.
5. Plutarch, *Isis and Osiris*, trans. Frank C. Babbitt. Cambridge, MA: Harvard University Press, 1936, pp. 37, 39.
6. Plutarch, *Isis and Osiris*, p. 45.
7. Lewis Spence, *Ancient Egyptian Myths and Legends*. New York: Dover, 1990, p. 166.
8. Quoted in Josephine Mayer and Tom Prideaux, eds., *Never to Die: The Egyptians in Their Own Words*. New York: Viking, 1938, p. 82.

Chapter Two: Ancient Greece

9. Edith Hamilton, *Mythology*. New York: Grand Central, 1999, p. 64.
10. Hamilton, *Mythology*, p. 18.
11. Michael Grant and John Hazel, *Who's Who in Classical Mythology*. London: Routledge, 2002, p. 250.
12. Grant and Hazel, *Who's Who in Classical Mythology*, p. 250.
13. Ovid, *Metamorphoses*, trans. Mary M. Innes. London: Penguin, 2006, p. 226.
14. Homer, *Odyssey*, trans. E.V. Rieu. Baltimore: Penguin, 1946, p. 329.

Chapter Three: Ancient Rome

15. Quoted in Theoi Greek Mythology, "Aphrodite Loves 2." www.theoi.com.

16. Virgil, *Aeneid*, trans. Patric Dickinson. New York: New American Library, 2002, p. 27.
17. Virgil, *Aeneid*, p. 97.
18. Virgil, *Aeneid*, p. 98.
19. Livy, *Livy: The Early History of Rome*, trans. Aubrey de Sélincourt. New York: Penguin, 2002, pp. 42–43.
20. Livy, *The Early History of Rome*, p. 44.
21. Apuleius, *The Golden Ass*, trans. P.G. Walsh, p. 76.
22. Apuleius, *The Golden Ass*, p. 81.

Chapter Four: Ancient India

23. Sowmya Rajendran, "Yama's Son Outwits the God of Death, Part 3," *New Indian Express* (Chennai, India), July 22, 2015. www.newindianexpress.com.
24. Subhamoy Das, "Immortal Love Legends: Romantic Tales from Hindu Literature," Learn Religions, 2019. www.learnreligions.com.
25. Kavita Kane, "Rediscovering 10 Intense Love Stories from Indian Mythology," She the People, November 5, 2018. www.shethepeople.tv.
26. Quoted in Swadharma, "Puranic Stories: Sanjana and Surya," June 21, 2019. https://swadharmastories.wordpress.com.
27. Magik India, "Radhakrishna, the Symbol of Divine Love," February 17, 2020. https://magikindia.com.

Chapter Five: Ancient China

28. Mae Hamilton, "Chang'e," Mythopedia, 2019. https://mythopedia.com.
29. Quoted in World Stories, "The Story of Niu Lang and Zhi Nu." https://worldstories.org.uk.
30. Shen Yun Performing Arts, "The Story of Liang and Zhu," 2021. www.shenyunperformingarts.org.

Books

Matt Clayton, *Hindu Mythology*. Charleston, SC: Amazon Digital Services, 2018.

Tammy Gagne, *Chinese Gods, Heroes, and Mythology*. Minneapolis, MN: ABDO, 2019.

Virginia Loh-Hagan, *Isis*. North Mankato, MN: 45th Parallel, 2019.

Don Nardo, *Gods of World Mythology*. San Diego, CA: ReferencePoint, 2022.

Katerina Servi, *Greek Mythology: Gods & Heroes: The Trojan War and The Odyssey*. Baton Rouge, LA: Third Millennium, 2018.

David Stuttard, *Roman Mythology: A Traveler's Guide from Troy to Tivoli*. London: Thames & Hudson, 2019.

Stephen E. Thompson, *Ancient Egypt: Facts and Fictions*. Santa Barbara, CA: ABC-CLIO, 2019.

Internet Sources

Saugat Adhikari, "Top 10 Astonishing Ancient Chinese Mythology Stories," Ancient History Lists, 2019. www.ancienthistorylists.com.

All That's Interesting, "44 Ancient Egypt Facts That Separate Myth from Truth," 2017. https://allthatsinteresting.com.

Subhamoy Das, "10 of the Most Important Hindu Gods," ThoughtCo, 2019. www.thoughtco.com.

Ducksters, "Ancient China: Mythology," 2019. www.ducksters.com.

Hinduwebsite.com, "Brahman: The Supreme Self," 2019. www.hinduwebsite.com.

Isaac Ogbodo, "Nigerian History: The Forgotten Gods of Igbo Culture." 2019. https://medium.com/african-history-collections/the-forgotten-gods -of-igbo-land-3030771eaf8b.

Rick Riordan, "Meet the Egyptian Gods." http://rickriordan.com.

Donald L. Wasson, "Roman Mythology," Ancient History Encyclopedia, 2018. www.ancient.eu.

Kuan L. Yong, "108 Chinese Mythological Gods and Characters to Know About," Owlcation, 2019. https://owlcation.com.

Websites

Ancient Egypt Site
www.ancient-egypt.org
Belgian Egyptologist Jacques Kinnaer writes and updates the text of the many pages of this colorful presentation of ancient Egyptian history and culture.

The Gods of Chinese Mythology, Godchecker
www.godchecker.com/chinese-mythology
Conceived by the late modern mythologist Chas Saunders, this informational site explains the best-known ancient Chinese gods in a well-designed, eye-catching format.

Hinduism, History.com
www.history.com/topics/religion/hinduism#section_3
One of the best overall websites on the internet about Hinduism, this site offers the basic facts behind Hindu gods, beliefs, sacred writings, rituals, and much more.

Theoi Greek Mythology
www.theoi.com
This is the most comprehensive and reliable general website about Greek mythology or the internet. It features hundreds of separate pages filled with detailed, accurate information, as well as numerous primary sources and reproductions of ancient paintings and mosaics.

INDEX

Cover: Guru Ji Creation/Shutterstock.com